WHAT MAKES GOD CRY THE MOST

(Things You Really Should Know About Abortion)

JIM HARRISON

PRESS

What Makes God Cry The Most
(Things You Really Should Know About Abortion)
by Jim Harrison

Printed in the United States of America

ISBN 978-1-60647-924-7

www.xulonpress.com

For each and every unborn child

Contents

My Word to You

Abortion is a subject which can be difficult to write about, and difficult to read about. In putting together this writing, my purpose has been to inform you so that you have a good understanding of important facts, and are better able to form your own opinions for decisions you may have to make. This is what you need to know.

It's clear even from the title that my own choice would be that of life. However, I value everyone equally, whether pro-life or pro-choice in outlook, and whether one has already counseled or had an abortion, or provided an abortion. [Of course, you could be pro-choice in view, and still choose life for your baby.]

I've tried to be completely honest and accurate in presenting information, and I have not included words or pictures intended to shock or disturb you.

I hope you find this worthwhile, and I ask that you read it with an open mind and an open heart.

Jim Harrison

1

The Unborn Child
is a Person

*Human life is sacred. . . From its very inception it
reveals the creating hand of God.[1]*
—POPE JOHN XXIII

I mean the unborn child is a person in the ordinary
sense of the word.[2] That is, an unborn child is a
human being, and she or he is a human being from
the time of conception,[3] the successful result of the
process of fertilization at which the nuclei of the
female ovum and the male sperm dynamically interact
or merge.[4] This is the time pregnancy begins.[5]

The individual ovum from the mother (which
contains 23 chromosomes) and sperm from the father
(which contains 23 chromosomes) cease to exist at
this point.[6] Instead a conceptus is formed which is a
new, although tiny, individual with a human genetic

code with its own genomic sequence (with 46 chromosomes), which is neither the mother's nor the father's.[7] From this point on, through the entire life of this new human being, no more genetic information is needed.[8] All of the inherited characteristics of this very special and unique person are in place. Our new person's gender, eye color, bone structure, hair color, skin color, susceptibility to certain diseases, and so on have been established.[9] The miracle of life has occurred and begun. It is an established scientific fact that all life, including human life, begins at the moment of conception.[10]

Throughout the entire pregnancy this embryo, later to be called a fetus, will be fulfilling her or his important function of growing within the warmth and comfort of the mother's womb. All that is necessary for this unborn child's growth and development is oxygen, food, water, and healthy interaction with the natural environment.[11] That's not so different from the rest of us. Although the embryo or fetus is in an earlier stage of development, and is living in a very special and protected place, we all need oxygen, food, water, and a congenial environment to grow and thrive and continue.

This baby is not just a part of the mother's body; she or he is a human being separate and distinct, but very much dependent, upon the mother. The unborn child is her or his own person doing exactly what this child is supposed to be doing at this time of life. The place of residence for now is within the mother's womb, and wonderful bonds can develop between the mother and child during the time of pregnancy.

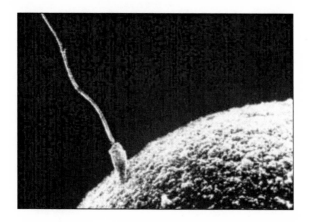

A Sperm Cell Fertilizing an Ovum

2

Life is a Miracle

Life is a miracle beyond our comprehension,
and we should reverence it. . .[1]
— C. J. BRIEJER

I t may be hard for us to understand how miraculous
life really is because our knowledge, although
increasing, is still quite limited; and because we
ourselves are living in and are part of that miracle.
In talking about the zygote, the one-celled brand
new human being formed upon conception, Bart
T. Heffernan, M.D., in "The Early Biography of
Everyman," tells us:

> The new combination of chromosomes [i.e.,
> the zygote's genetic structure] sets in motion
> the individual's life, controlled by his own
> individual code (genes) with its fantastic
> library of information projected from the past

on the helix of. . . DNA. A single thread of DNA from a human cell contains information equivalent to six hundred thousand printed pages with five hundred words on a page, or a library of one thousand volumes. The stored knowledge at conception in the new individual's library of instruction is fifty times more than that contained in the *Encyclopedia Britannica*. These unique and individual instructions are operative over the whole of the individual's life and form a continuum of human existence even into succeeding generations.[2]

This look at the beginning human being focuses on the information and instructions contained in the one-celled person. Think about how incredible this is. One cell that is smaller than a grain of sugar,[3] much smaller than a period on this page,[4] contains fifty times more information than that contained in a complete set of *Encyclopedia Britannica*. And it links the past, no matter how far back that goes, with the future, no matter how far forward that will go.

The more than 20,000 genes in the human genome are the units of heredity.[5] They are biochemical instructions that tell cells, the basic units of life, how to manufacture certain proteins.[6] Through a variety of mechanisms, a single gene may give rise to many proteins.[7] And these proteins control the characteristics that create much of our individuality, from our hair and eye color, to the shapes of our body parts, to our talents, personality traits, and health.[8]

These genes are present in totality in the one-celled zygote.[9] And they are all present in every cell, except red blood cells, of the trillions of cells of this human being's body as it develops and goes through life; however, cells differ in appearance and function because they use only some of their genes.[10] Some traits and illnesses are determined by single genes.[11] Most genes do not function alone but are influenced by the actions of other genes, as well as by factors in the environment.[12]

A look at human life from other points of view would also be stunning. Areas of science that are deeply involved in trying to understand human life include molecular biology, biochemistry, embryology, genetics, behavioral sciences, and others. Advanced technologies, engineering, and sophisticated computer and mathematical and statistical techniques support their investigations. And ethical issues and moral principles have an important role in all we do. **We're not even close to comprehending the complexities of life. Life is special, and we're special, and the developing baby in the mother's womb is special. And this miracle is happening around us all the time.**

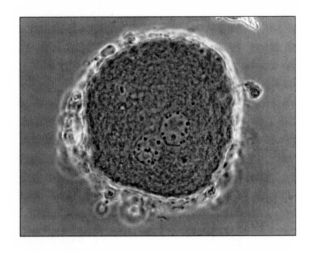

**Nuclei of the Sperm and Ovum Dynamically Interact
to Form a Zygote**

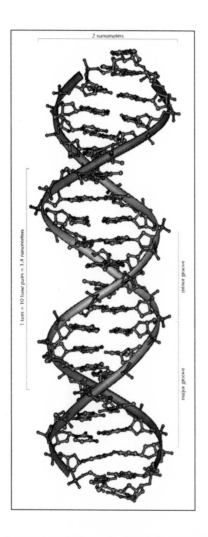

The Structure of Part of a DNA Double Helix

3

Development of Your Baby

*Even if our own mouths were as full of song
as the sea, and our lips as full of praise as the
breadths of the heaven,
and our eyes as bright as the sun, and
our hands as outstretched as the eagles of the sky,
and our feet as swift as gazelles,
we could not thank You enough.[1]*
—MICHAL SMART

It's amazing. The growth and development of the baby which takes place during the nine months in the mother's womb is far greater than at any other time of life. What happens, and how it happens, is beyond our most wild imagination. We could never come up with something like this.

The length of pregnancy is most accurately considered to be 266 days, or 38 weeks, after fertilization.[2] The baby is called an embryo from the moment of fertilization until the end of the eighth week (the first eight weeks of human development). During the first two weeks the baby increases in number of cells and travels to and becomes implanted in the womb, which is a protected place to grow. The third to the eighth week is the period during which each of three primary layers of cells begins to grow into specialized parts of the body, including among others the digestive system, liver, lungs, heart, sex organs, bones, kidneys, muscles, nervous system, hair, skin, and eyes.[3] As a result of organ formation, major features of body form are established. After that until birth the baby is called a fetus. And during this time from the beginning of the ninth week until birth, the tissues and organs of the child mature, and there is rapid growth of the body.

Development of the baby is a highly regulated program of genetic switches that are turned on in specific body parts at specific times.[4] A set of genes controls how the embryo develops its parts in the right places.[5] As the days and weeks of development proceed, different rates of cell division in different parts of the embryo fold the forming tissues into intricate patterns. In a process called embryonic induction, the specialization of one group of cells causes adjacent groups of cells to specialize. Gradually, these changes mold the three primary germ layers into organs and organ systems.[6]

Some things happen so quickly that it seems remarkable. The future sex cells that will give rise to sperm or eggs for a new generation, that's the generation after this one, begin to group together, only 17 days after this new life is alive itself.[7] At approximately three weeks after conception, the baby is about the size of an orange seed, and its heart is about the size of a poppy seed, and the heart has already begun to beat, starting at a rate of about 70 times per minute and increasing later.[8] At less than four weeks old, the lungs begin to form.[9] At around six weeks, electrical activity is detectable in the brain, although it has most probably begun before that.[10]

At eight weeks, the baby is well-proportioned, and about the size of a thumb. Every organ is present. The liver is making blood, the kidneys function, and the heart beats steadily. The skull, elbows, and knees are forming. The skeleton of the arms and legs and the spine begins to stiffen as bone cells are added.[11] At 10 weeks the baby's fingernails begin to develop.[12] At 11 weeks the baby can make complex facial expressions and even smile.[13] At 12 weeks the baby sucks its thumb and practices breathing,[14] since she or he will have to breathe air immediately after birth. At 13 weeks facial expressions may even resemble those of the parents. The baby is active, but Mom doesn't feel anything yet.[15] At 15 weeks the baby is practicing sucking and swallowing to get ready for breast or bottle feeding.[16] Before four months the baby will have her or his own unique fingerprints.[17] Before five months, because rapid eye movement (REM) is occurring, the baby is likely dreaming.[18] At five months Mom may feel her baby kick, turn or hiccup and may be able to identify a bulge as an elbow or head.[19]

At just over six months the baby will be able to hear.[20] She or he can listen, learn,[21] and remember.

The baby responds differently to her or his mother's voice compared with others, and the baby prefers the mother's voice as it would sound through amniotic fluid. (As a newborn, the baby responds with a calmer heart rate when read a story she or he heard often in the womb.) The child sleeps and wakes, nestling in her or his favorite positions to sleep, and stretches upon waking.[22] At eight months the pupils of the eye respond to light, and it's really getting crowded in there.[23] The baby triggers labor and birth occurs an average of 264 – 270 days after conception. And not until all of these things have occurred on the inside, can we see the new child on the outside.[24]

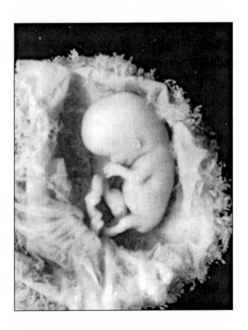

Eight-Week-Old Embryo

21 Week Fetus Grasping Hand of Surgeon

4

The Way We Think

There is one thing that every individual can do,
—they can see to it that they feel right.
An atmosphere of sympathetic influence encircles
every human being; and the man or woman
who feels strongly, healthily, and justly,
on the great interests of humanity,
is a constant benefactor to the human race.[1]
—HARRIET BEECHER STOWE

We've got a problem. It's the way we sometimes think about things.

There are many reasons parents have or have given for considering whether there is room in their lives or on this earth for their unborn child.

They may feel that they are too young, or they're going to school, they were just having fun, have parents who don't understand, are not married, or want to have a life without the complications of a child.

They may have just wanted to see if they could get pregnant, wanted to force their partners to take the relationship more seriously, wanted to force their partners into marriage, perhaps don't want to add stress to the relationship, don't want others to know that they were having sex or got pregnant, or don't want the child in the way of finding their eventual life partners.

They may feel their lives are so demanding already, they're so busy, they're working, they have careers, they don't have the time or energy, they're married with other children who need their care, they need more money, the new child would be a financial burden, they can't see the unborn child, they don't want to admit that the child in the womb is a special human being already with the possibility of a full and wonderful life ahead of her or him.

They may feel they are too old, that the new child is inconvenient, the child may not be born perfect, they're significant others don't want the child, the law gives them the right, they can do what they want with their bodies, there are too many people in the world anyway, that there is just no room on earth for this new baby.

We can't help it. It's human nature to some extent to focus our decisions on ourselves and what we perceive at the time to be in our best interests. Sometimes we who are products of our own circumstances, our culture, our times, and our laws can be unaware of or become desensitized to the plight of others. In this case we may even become less feeling of our own unborn child, who is so dependent on us for her or his continued existence and opportunity to live its life. In the next chapter, I show some similarities between slavery at an earlier time and abortion today. It all comes down to the way we think; the way of thinking which allowed slavery to exist and continue for so long, is similar to how we are sustaining abortion today.

More thought, imagination and determination would show us that by taking the pregnancy to term and allowing the baby to live, life would be better for us and a full life would be possible for the new child. We just have to know and understand the possibilities of keeping the child or using adoptive services, and to get the right kind of support and help when we need it. There are a lot of people and organizations who want to help. **The only really bad result is the death of the child, and there are many ways to make sure that doesn't happen.**

5

The Law

*Once we come to the recognition that any act stands
in the class of a wrong. . . the logic of that
recognition forbids us from treating that act
any longer as a matter of personal taste
or private choice.[1]*
—HADLEY ARKES

Our legal system is extremely important to all
of us, and our federal judiciary is fantastic. We
citizens of this great country are incredibly fortunate
to live under our Constitution and to have in place
the federal district courts, appellate courts, and the
United States Supreme Court to keep everything in
line with our important principles. The judges and
justices of our federal courts are among the best of
the best this country has to offer. Their intellect,
personal standards, and patriotism are of the highest
order and serve as models for the rest of us.

But they, just like the rest of us, are persons of their time and of our culture. And they make mistakes sometimes. And then it takes a while for them and us to fix what we later come to understand are poor decisions.

At the Supreme Court level, consider *Dred Scott v. Sandford* (1857)[2], which dealt with slavery and held that black people have no rights that white people are bound to respect. Or *Plessy v. Ferguson* (1896)[3], which affirmed the constitutionality of legally enforced racial segregation. Or *Korematsu v. United States* (1944)[4], which affirmed the wartime right to exclude American citizens of Japanese ancestry from a west coast area in which their homes were located. Today we look back at these decisions with horror; but then, when they were decided, they made sense to a lot of people, including the justices who decided them.

We can't always count on poor decisions being overturned by the court. Sometimes even poor decisions don't become explicitly overturned, and *Korematsu* is a good example of that. However, as legal precedent, *Korematsu* is recognized as having very limited application.[5] The court can diminish poor decisions without overturning them.

There are strong similarities between how we used to treat blacks in our country, and how we treat our unborn children today. Today we look at racial prejudices and slavery in particular as absolutely monstrous and inhumane. But not at an earlier time. Think about whether we thought of blacks then, and unborn children now, as property or as individuals who should be protected by the law. In the *Dred Scott* case in 1857, the United States Supreme Court declared that all blacks, slaves as well as free, were not and could never become citizens of the United States. In addition, the Court declared provisions of the Missouri Compromise unconstitutional, thus permitting slavery in all of the country's territories. The Court also implied that the framers of the Constitution believed that blacks "had no rights which the white man was bound to respect; and that the negro might justly and lawfully be reduced to slavery for his benefit. He was bought and sold and treated as an ordinary article of merchandise and traffic, whenever profit could be made by it." It took a long time and a lot of legislation, and Constitutional amendment, to dig our way out of that awful place. It also took changing perceptions and understandings, *Uncle Tom's Cabin*[6] by Harriet Beecher Stowe, and a Civil War to get things right.

Leaving out the war part, we seem to be going through some similar struggles with matters concerning protection of the unborn child. We've got *Roe v. Wade* (1973)[7] which had the immediate effect of nullifying nearly every state abortion law in the country, and additional court decisions and legislation which have followed to interpret and qualify and limit *Roe*. And the United States Supreme Court which does not consider an unborn child fully developed and just moments before being born, a "person" under the Constitution;[8] even as the courts constructively or fictionally consider a corporation which is not even a human being, a person within the meaning of the equal protection and due process provisions of the Constitution.[9]

Sometimes the law just says what we can get away with. That's the way it was with slavery. And that's the way it is with abortion.

We can't always look to the law to help us decide what is right to do or what we should do. We need to look to our consciences, our families, our friends who are mature and have wisdom and care about us, and our places of worship for that.

Slave Trade Auction Block

Japanese American WWII Internment Camp

6

Abortion Methods

Now imagine such a democracy, in which women
would be valued so very highly. . .
In that world we might well describe the unborn
and the never-to-be-born with the honest
words of life. And in that world, passionate
feminists might well hold candlelight vigils
at abortion clinics, standing shoulder
to shoulder with the doctors who work there,
commemorating and saying goodbye to the dead.[1]
—NAOMI WOLF

Make no mistake about it, abortion is violent. All induced abortion methods involve killing of a human being, and that just doesn't happen without trauma to the body of the child. Below are brief descriptions of some abortion methods. Although it is not my intent to disturb you, the factual descriptions may be troubling. If you understand the first two sentences of this paragraph and if the details of abortion methods make you feel uncomfortable, just move on to the next chapter. You already know a lot.

Dismember the baby.

Suction Curettage or Suction-Aspiration. This is the method of abortion which is most commonly used in first trimester abortions.[2] The cervical muscle ring must be paralyzed and stretched open. The abortionist then inserts a hollow plastic tube with a knife-like edge into the uterus. The suction tears the baby's soft body into pieces. The placenta is cut from the uterine wall and everything is sucked into a bottle.[3]

Dilation and Curettage (D&C). This is similar to a suction procedure except a curette, a loop-shaped steel knife is inserted into the uterus. The baby and placenta are cut into pieces and scraped out into a basin. Bleeding is usually very heavy with this method.[4]

Dilation and Evacuation (D&E). This type of abortion is done after the third month of pregnancy. The cervix must be dilated before the abortion. Usually Laminaria sticks are inserted into the cervix. These are made of sterilized seaweed that is compressed into thin sticks. When inserted, they absorb moisture and expand, thus enlarging the cervix. A pliers-like instrument is inserted through the cervix into the uterus. The abortionist then seizes a leg, arm or other part of the baby and, with a twisting motion, tears it from the body. This continues until only the head remains. Finally the skull is crushed and pulled out. The nurse must then reassemble the body parts to be sure that all of them were removed.[5]

Poison and burn the baby.

Salt Poisoning (Saline Injection). A long needle is inserted into the mother's abdomen.[6] A concentrated salt solution is injected into the amniotic fluid in which the baby lives. The solution is absorbed by the unborn child through both the lungs and the gastro-intestinal tract, poisoning the baby. In addition, the outer layer of skin is burned off by the high concentration of salt. It takes about an hour to kill the baby by this slow method. The mother usually goes into labor about a day later and delivers a dead, shriveled baby, if it is a post 16-week saline abortion.[7]

Methotrexate. This is a chemical abortion in which a woman receives an injection of methotrexate, a poison which kills the developing baby. About five days later she inserts misoprostol tablets into her vagina. The pregnancy usually ends at home within a day or two, although 15-20 percent of women undergoing this procedure require up to four weeks to terminate their pregnancies successfully. The baby and other products of conception that develop during pregnancy are passed out through the vagina.[8]

Starve and suffocate the baby.

Mifepristone (RU-486). This works by blocking progesterone, a crucial hormone during pregnancy.

Without progesterone, the uterine lining does not provide food, fluid and oxygen to the tiny developing baby. The baby cannot survive.[9] In a few days the mother uses a second medication, misoprostol. The pregnancy usually ends within four hours after taking the misoprostol. The baby and other products of conception that develop during pregnancy are passed out through the vagina.[10]

Perform a hysterectomy and let the baby die.

Hysterectomy. This is similar to a Cesarean Section which is usually performed to save the life of the baby. Except that in an abortion, the baby is alive but allowed to die through neglect or sometimes killed by a direct act.[11]

Vacuum the brain from the baby.

Dilation and Extraction (D&X) or "Partial-Birth Abortion." Using ultrasound, the abortionist grips the baby's legs with forceps. The unborn child is then pulled out through the birth canal and delivered with the exception of its head. While the head is in the womb the abortionist penetrates the live baby's skull with scissors, opens the scissors to enlarge the hole, and then inserts a catheter. The baby's brain is vacuumed out, resulting in the skull's collapse. The abortionist then completes the womb's evacuation by removing a dead baby.[12] There is now a federal ban on partial-birth abortion which is enforceable nationwide.[13]

Induce labor too early for the baby to survive.

Prostaglandin. Prostaglandin is a hormone that induces labor.[14] The abortionist may insert prostaglandin into the vagina or give the medication in the form of an injection to start contractions that will expel the baby.[15] The baby usually dies from the trauma of the delivery. To further ensure that the baby is not born alive, some abortionists use ultrasound to guide them as they inject a drug into the unborn baby's heart to kill the baby. They then administer prostaglandin and a dead baby is delivered. This type of abortion is used in mid- and late-term pregnancies.[16]

Prevent implantation of the new baby.

Intrauterine Device (IUD). The IUD is a small plastic or metal device that is inserted through the vagina and into the cavity of the uterus. In some cases the IUD may prevent fertilization. However, when fertilization does occur, its effect is to prevent the implantation of the tiny new human being into the nutrient lining of the uterus, and effectively kill the baby at one week of life.[17]

Morning-after Pill. This causes a hardening of the lining of the uterus, which prevents implantation of the new human being. In some cases the morning-after pill might act in a sterilizing fashion by preventing an ovulation, and fertilization doesn't occur.[18]

7

Unborn Babies Feel Pain

> *By acquiescing in an act that can cause such*
> *suffering to a living creature, who among us*
> *is not diminished as a human being?[1]*
> —RACHEL CARSON

We've come a long way. In 1973, when *Roe v. Wade* was handed down, we knew very little about life in the womb. Today, technology allows us to detect brain waves as early as six weeks, to see into the womb through ultrasound and, through fetal surgery, to correct disabling conditions that a number of years ago would have condemned a child to an early death.[2]

There is a lot of authority for the understanding that unborn babies feel pain, and particularly so when they are the victims of abortion. In open fetal surgery, in which a pregnant woman's uterus is cut open and the fetus exposed, surgeons have seen tiny

25-week-old fetuses recoil in what looks like pain when the scalpel is lowered to them.[3] Surgeons have observed 23-week-old fetuses flinching at the touch of the instrument.[4] New evidence has persuaded many doctors that fetuses can feel pain by 20 weeks gestation (that is, halfway through a full-term pregnancy) and possibly earlier.[5] Some research has shown that fetuses as young as 18 weeks react to an invasive procedure with a spike in stress hormones and a shunting of blood flow toward the brain – a strategy, also seen in infants and adults, to protect a vital organ from threat.[6]

Although the cerebral cortex, which is believed to be the organ of consciousness, is not fully developed in the fetus until late in gestation, a structure called the subplate zone is up and running and some scientists believe this may be capable of processing pain signals.[7] A kind of holding station for developing nerve cells, which eventually melds into the mature brain, the subplate zone becomes operational at about 17 weeks.[8] There is also some opinion that the brain stem itself can support consciousness and the experience of pain and, like the subplate zone, is active in the fetus far earlier than the cerebral cortex.[9] The fetus's undeveloped state, in other words, may not preclude it from feeling pain. In fact, its immature physiology may well make it more sensitive to pain, not less, because the body's mechanisms for inhibiting pain and making it more bearable do not become active until after birth.[10]

Then there's the ultrasound video tape and movie of a suction abortion of a 12-week unborn child. This shows the unborn baby dodging the suction instrument time after time, while its heartbeat doubles in rate. When finally caught, its body being dismembered, the baby's mouth clearly opens wide.[11]

At ten weeks, if the baby's forehead is touched, she or he may turn its head away.[12] At nine weeks, the entire body is sensitive to touch, except the sides, back, and top of the head.[13] At eight and a half weeks, if the eyelid is stroked, the child squirms.[14] If the palm is stroked, the child's fingers close into a small fist.[15] At seven weeks, the nervous system is well developed.[16] If the area of the lips is stroked, the child responds by bending her or his upper body to one side and making a quick backward motion with a hand.[17]

Even though the unborn can not yet speak to us with words, they do speak to us through what we see during fetal surgery, our increasing knowledge of the development of structures that may process pain signals, and the babies' reactions and movements upon being aborted or even touched. **We need to understand that unborn babies feel pain, and in some cases they may suffer terribly during abortion procedures.**

8

Problems After an Abortion

*I am convinced that every abortion
is an unplanned tragedy, brought about by a
combination of human errors. . .[1]*
—JIMMY CARTER

Abortion can change your life in ways you wish it hadn't. Although the father, grandparents, and other family members and friends may be truly affected, the mother of the baby can be hit the hardest. For her, there may be immediate complications from the procedure, longer term medical issues including her ability to bear healthy children in the future, and a number of near-term and long-term psychological problems including depression and post-traumatic stress disorder.[2]

The most common major physical complications which can occur at the time of an abortion are infection, excessive bleeding, embolism, ripping or perforation of the uterus, anesthesia complications, convulsions, hemorrhage, cervical injury, and endotoxic shock.[3] The most common minor complications are lesser infections, bleeding, fever, second degree burns, chronic abdominal pain, vomiting, gastrointestinal disturbances, and Rh sensitization.[4]

While the immediate complications of abortion are usually treatable, these complications may lead to long-term reproductive damage of much more serious nature.[5] For example, one possible outcome of abortion-related infections is sterility.[6] Also, women who acquire post-abortion infections are more likely to experience ectopic pregnancies later (in which the fertilized ovum develops outside the uterus, as in a fallopian tube).[7] Cervical damage from previously induced abortions increases the risk of miscarriage, premature birth, and complications of labor during later pregnancies.[8] In addition, premature births, complications of labor, and abnormal development of the placenta, all of which can result from latent abortion morbidity, are leading causes of handicaps such as cerebral palsy and fetal malformation among the newborns post-abortive women may have.[9] Other increased risks to the mother may include death, breast cancer, pelvic inflammatory disease, endometritis (inflammation of the inner lining of the uterus), and cervical, ovarian, and liver cancer.[10]

Women who have multiple abortions face a much greater risk of experiencing physical complications.[11] And teenagers are also at much higher risk of suffering many abortion-related complications, both immediate complications and long-term reproductive damage.[12]

Abortion has also been linked to increased mental health problems.[13] These may occur soon after an abortion, or after a number of years because many post-abortive women use repression or denial as a coping mechanism.[14] The mental health problems may include depression, nervous disorders, sleep disturbances, regrets about the decision, self-destructive behavior and feelings of self-hatred, sexual dysfunction, thoughts of suicide and attempted suicide, increased substance abuse (drugs, alcohol, and tobacco), eating disorders (binge eating, bulimia, and anorexia nervosa), child neglect or abuse of children born later, divorce and chronic relationship problems, and symptoms or even clinical diagnosis of post-traumatic stress disorder (in this context sometimes referred to as post-abortion syndrome).[15]

Women who have had abortions are more likely than others to later become admitted to a psychiatric hospital.[16] Particularly vulnerable to post-traumatic stress and other problems are women who have been coerced or forced into unwanted abortions.[17] As with physical complications, teenagers who have had an abortion are at especially high risk for mental health problems.[18]

There are many roles that the baby's father may have played in the abortion, ranging from opposing the abortion, to not doing enough to prevent the abortion, to not knowing of or wanting the abortion, to being neutral on the abortion decision, to supporting the abortion decision, to abandoning the mother in the face of pregnancy, to coercing the mother to have the abortion.[19] Like the mother, the father may become affected immediately or years later.[20] Some of the feelings and reactions the baby's father may have include sadness, grief, guilt, anger, sense of not being able to protect, holding himself responsible, drug abuse, and alcohol abuse.[21]

9

Help and Support

*I believe we can all recognize that abortion
in many ways represents a sad, even tragic choice
to many, many women.[1]*
—HILLARY RODHAM CLINTON

Help and support are closer than you think.
There are nearly 4,000 pro-life pregnancy help
centers in the United States.[2] A typical center employs
one or two qualified social workers and has, in addition, 10 to 50 or more volunteers.[3] Approximately 98
percent of the staff is female.[4] Some of the services
these centers may offer include a 24-hour helpline,
pregnancy testing, pregnancy options counseling,
ultrasound examinations, parenting support, mate-
rial aid, referrals for community services including
medical and housing, adoption support, mentoring,
after abortion support, STD/STI (sexually transmitted

disease/sexually transmitted infection) information and testing, and men's programs.[5]

There is a lot of help available through wonderful organizations and people who believe that your and your baby's welfare is of the highest importance. It means a lot that the people in these pro-life pregnancy centers who are so concerned about helping so that your baby will be born, are the same people who do the most to help women and men heal after they have had or supported or been affected by an abortion. They are sincere in their belief of the value of your and your baby's lives. You may even benefit from talking to a post-abortive woman who has come to regret her decision and is now serving to help other women make their decision.

This is how easy it is to find a pregnancy center near you, and get contact information. Just call 1-800-395-HELP anytime, 24 hours a day, 7 days a week; or go online to www.pregnancycenters.org, click on Find a Center, key in your zip code, and then click on the Find Location button. This will give you nearby centers with addresses, telephone numbers, hours and services.[6]

So, before you begin down the path of considering an abortion, contact a pregnancy center and discuss your problems and concerns and options with someone who cares. This is a life or death decision for your baby with serious implications for you as well. Also, talk to others you can trust – your partner, your parents, a minister, a priest, a rabbi, an imam or other faith representative, or perhaps a good friend. Become informed; and listen to your conscience. Choosing to continue your pregnancy and to parent is very challenging. But with the support of caring people, parenting classes, and other resources, many women find the help they need to make this choice. You may also decide to place your child for adoption. This loving decision is often made by women who first thought abortion was the only option in their circumstances.

It may even be possible for you to see your baby with an ultrasound examination available at a growing number of the pregnancy centers. This is a simple screening test which uses sound waves of such high frequency they can't be heard by the human ear.[7] There are no known risks and many benefits which have been associated with the use of ultrasound.[8] You may be able to spot your baby's beating heart; the curve of the spine; the face, arms, and legs.[9] You may even catch sight of your baby sucking its thumb.[10] And it may also be possible to determine whether the baby is a girl or a boy.[11]

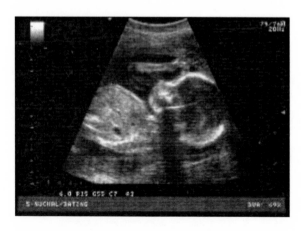

Ultrasound of 22 Week Fetus

10

Choosing Life

*Love your children without reserve
for they are a joy and a miracle.*[1]
—EVAN CLARK

One of the most important things to remember is that your unborn baby is a whole, separate, unique living human being from the time of conception.[2] Your unborn child is her or his own person growing within the warmth and comfort of the mother's womb and doing exactly what this child is supposed to be doing at this time of life. And life really is a miracle much more special and complex than we can comprehend at this time. The amount of growth and development that takes place during the nine months in the mother's womb, and how it all happens, is an amazing process that is something we could never imagine or come up with on our own. All human life should be greatly valued in all its stages, not for what we do, but for what we are.[3]

There are many reasons parents have for considering whether there is room in their lives for their unborn child. But more thought, imagination and determination would show us that by taking the pregnancy to term and allowing the baby to have its opportunity to live, life would be better for us and a full life would be possible for the new child. We just have to know and understand the possibilities of keeping the child or using adoptive services, and to get the right kind of support and help when we need it. The only really bad result is the death of the child, and there are many ways to make sure that doesn't happen. Even though the law may allow us to seek an abortion under some circumstances, we can't always look to the law to help us decide what is right to do or what we should do. We need to look to our consciences, our families, our friends who are mature and have wisdom and care about us, and our places of worship for that.

We should keep in mind how violent abortion really is. All induced abortion methods involve killing of a human being, and that just doesn't happen without trauma to the body of the child. We need to understand that unborn babies feel pain, and in some cases they may suffer terribly during abortion procedures. And abortion can change your life in ways you wish it hadn't. Although the father, grandparents, and other family members and friends may be truly affected, the mother of the baby can be hit the hardest. For her, there may be immediate complications from the procedure, longer term medical issues including her ability to bear healthy children in the future, and a number of near-term and long-term psychological problems including depression and post-traumatic stress disorder.

There are many pro-life pregnancy health centers in the United States. They are staffed by people who believe that your and your baby's welfare is of the highest importance. And pregnancy centers near you can be found by calling1-800-395-HELP or going online to www.pregnancycenters.org. So, before you begin down the path of considering an abortion, contact a pregnancy center and discuss your problems and concerns and options with someone who cares. This is a life or death decision for your baby with serious implications for you as well. You may even be able to see your baby with an ultrasound examination available at a growing number of the pregnancy centers, and benefit from talking to a post-abortive woman who has come to regret her decision and is now serving to help other women make their decision. Also, talk to others you can trust – your partner, your parents, a minister, a priest, a rabbi, an imam or other faith representative, or perhaps a good friend. Become informed; and listen to your conscience.

Choosing to continue your pregnancy and to parent is very challenging. But with the support of caring people, parenting classes, and other resources, many women find the help they need to make this choice. You may also decide to place your child for adoption. This loving decision is

**often made by women who first thought abortion
was the only option in their circumstances.**[4]

I hope you choose life.

Notes

Chapter 1. The Unborn Child is a Person

1. Pope John XXIII as cited in *Human Vitae* (On Human Life), Encyclical Letter by Pope Paul VI, July 25, 1968.

2. *Webster's New World College Dictionary*, 4th Edition (Cleveland: Wiley Publishing, Inc., 2006). Definition of "person" as a "human being."

3. Francis J. Beckwith, *Defending Life, A Moral and Legal Case against Abortion Choice* (New York: Cambridge University Press, 2007), p. 65.

4. *Defending Life*, p. 66.

5. *Defending Life*, p. 66.

6. *Defending Life*, p. 66.

7. *Defending Life*, p. 67.

8. *Defending Life*, p. 67.

9. *Defending Life*, p. 67.

10. Dr. Hymie Gordon, professor of medical genetics and physician at the Mayo Clinic, as cited in *Defending Life*, p. 68.

11. *Defending Life*, p. 67-68.

Chapter 2. Life is a Miracle

1.   Dr. C. J. Briejer as cited by Rachel Carson in *Silent Spring*, 40th Anniversary Edition (New York: Houghton Mifflin Company, First Mariner Books Edition, 2002), p. 275.

2.   Bart T. Heffernan, M.D., as cited by Francis J. Beckwith in *Defending Life, A Moral and Legal Case against Abortion Choice* (New York: Cambridge University Press, 2007), p. 70.

3.   www.abortionfacts.com, *Milestones of Early Life*, Heritage House '76, Inc.

4.   Heidi Murkoff and Sharon Mazel, *What to Expect When You're Expecting*, 4th Edition (New York: Workman Publishing Company, 2008), p. 121.

5.   Ricki Lewis, *Human Genetics, Concepts and Applications*, 8th Edition (New York: McGraw-Hill, 2008), p. 2.

6.   *Human Genetics*, p. 2.

7.   T. W. Sadler, *Langman's Medical Embryology*, 10th Edition (Philadelphia: Lippincott Williams & Wilkins, 2006), p. 5.

8.   *Human Genetics*, p. 2.

9.   Francis J. Beckwith, *Defending Life, A Moral and Legal Case against Abortion Choice* (New York: Cambridge University Press, 2007), p. 67, 70. *Human Genetics*, p. 50.

10.   *Human Genetics*, p. 4.

11.   *Human Genetics*, p. 7.

12.   *Human Genetics*, p. 7.

Chapter 3. Development of Your Baby

1.   Michal Smart, a member of the Coalition on the Environment and Jewish Life, as cited in *Keeping the Earth: Religious and Scientific Perspectives on the Environment*.

2.   T. W. Sadler, *Langman's Medical Embryology*, 10th Edition (Philadelphia: Lippincott Williams & Wilkins, 2006), pp. 89, 90.

3.   Heidi Murkoff and Sharon Mazel, *What to Expect When You're Expecting*, 4th Edition (New York: Workman Publishing Company, 2008), p. 121.

4.   Ricki Lewis, *Human Genetics, Concepts and Applications*, 8th Edition (New York: McGraw-Hill, 2008), p. 60.

5.   *Human Genetics*, p. 53.

6.   *Human Genetics*, p. 56.

7.   www.abortionfacts.com, *Milestones of Early Life*, Heritage House '76, Inc.

8.   *What to Expect*, pp. 150-151. *Milestones of Early Life*.

9.   *Milestones of Early Life*.

10. Francis J. Beckwith, *Defending Life, A Moral and Legal Case against Abortion Choice* (New York: Cambridge University Press, 2007), p. 71.

11. *Milestones of Early Life*.

12. *Milestones of Early Life*.

13. *Milestones of Early Life*.

14. *Human Genetics*, p. 57.

15. *Milestones of Early Life*.

16. *What to Expect*, p. 199.

17. *What to Expect*, p. 232.
18. *Defending Life*, p. 72.
19. *Milestones of Early Life*.
20. *Milestones of Early Life*.
21. *Defending Life*, p. 72.
22. *Milestones of Early Life*.
23. *Milestones of Early Life*.
24. *Milestones of Early Life*.

Chapter 4. The Way We Think

1. Harriet Beecher Stowe, *Uncle Tom's Cabin* (New York: Barnes & Noble Books, 2005), p. 438. [*Uncle Tom's Cabin* was serialized between 1851 and 1852, and published in volume form in 1852.]

Chapter 5. The Law

1. Hadley Arkes as cited by Francis J. Beckwith in *Defending Life, A Moral and Legal Case against Abortion Choice* (New York: Cambridge University Press, 2007), p. 16.
2. *Dred Scott v. Sandford*, 60 U.S. (19 How.) 393 (1857).
3. *Plessy v. Ferguson*, 163 U.S. 537 (1896).
4. *Korematsu v. United States*, 323 U.S. 214 (1944).
5. Judge Marilyn Hall Patel, U.S. District Court for the Northern District of California, 1984.
6. Harriet Beecher Stowe, *Uncle Tom's Cabin*. [*Uncle Tom's Cabin* was serialized between 1851 and 1852, and published in volume form in 1852.]

7. *Roe v. Wade*, 410 U.S. 113 (1973).

8. *Roe v. Wade*.

9. A corporation is a "person" within the meaning of equal protection and due process provisions of the United States Constitution. Allen v. Pavach, Ind., 335 N.E.2d 219, 221; Borreca v. Fasi, D.C.Hawaii, 369 F.Supp. 906, 911.

Chapter 6. Abortion Methods

1. Naomi Wolf, "Our Bodies, Our Souls," *The New Republic*, October 16, 1995. As included in Melody Rose, *Abortion, A Documentary and Reference Guide* (Westport, Connecticut: Greenwood Press, 2008), pp. 216-217.

2. www.abortionfacts.com, *Learn Abortion Facts*, Heritage House '76, Inc.

3. www.abortionfacts.com, *How Are Abortions Done?*, Heritage House '76, Inc.

4. *How Are Abortions Done?*

5. *How Are Abortions Done?*

6. *Learn Abortion Facts*.

7. Francis J. Beckwith, *Defending Life, A Moral and Legal Case against Abortion Choice* (New York: Cambridge University Press, 2007), pp. 87-88.

8. *Defending Life*, pp. 86-87.

9. *How Are Abortions Done?*

10. *Defending Life*, p. 87.

11. *Defending Life*, pp. 89, 91.

12. *Defending Life*, p. 88.

13. Partial-Birth Abortion Ban Act (P.L. 108-105). *Gonzales v. Carhart*, 550 U.S. ____ (2007).

14. *How Are Abortions Done?*

15. *Defending Life*, p. 87.

16. *How Are Abortions Done?*

17. John C. Willke and Barbara H. Willke, *Why Can't We Love Them Both, Questions and Answers about Abortion* (Cincinnati: Hayes Publishing Company, 1997), p. 127.

18. *Why Can't We Love Them Both*, p. 128.

Chapter 7. Unborn Babies Feel Pain

1. Rachel Carson, *Silent Spring*, 40th Anniversary Edition (New York: Houghton Mifflin Company, First Mariner Books Edition, 2002), p. 100.

2. Laura Echevarria, LifeNews.com Editor, *Abortion Backers Can't Ignore New York Times Story That Babies Feel Pain*, February 14, 2008.

3. Annie Murphy Paul, *The First Ache*, The New York Times, February 10, 2008.

4. *The First Ache.*

5. *The First Ache.*

6. *The First Ache.*

7. *The First Ache.*

8. *The First Ache.*

9. *The First Ache.*

10. *The First Ache.*

11. *The Silent Scream* DVD available from Heritage House '76 at www.heritagehouse76.com.

12. Francis J. Beckwith, *Defending Life, A Moral and Legal Case against Abortion Choice* (New York: Cambridge University Press, 2007), p. 90.

13. *Defending Life*, p. 90.

14. *Defending Life*, p. 90.
15. *Defending Life*, p. 90.
16. *Defending Life*, p. 90.
17. *Defending Life*, p. 90.

Chapter 8. Problems After an Abortion

1. Jimmy Carter, "Would Jesus Approve Abortions and the Death Penalty?," *Our Endangered Values*, 2005. As included in Melody Rose, *Abortion, A Documentary and Reference Guide* (Westport, Connecticut: Greenwood Press, 2008), p. 226.
2. www.afterabortion.org, Elliot Institute.
3. www.afterabortion.org.
4. www.afterabortion.org.
5. www.afterabortion.org.
6. www.afterabortion.org.
7. www.afterabortion.org.
8. www.afterabortion.org.
9. www.afterabortion.org.
10. www.afterabortion.org.
11. www.afterabortion.org.
12. www.afterabortion.org.
13. www.afterabortion.org.
14. www.afterabortion.org.
15. www.afterabortion.org.
16. www.afterabortion.org.
17. www.afterabortion.org.
18. www.afterabortion.org.
19. www.menandabortion.info, *Description of Aftermath – Impact of Abortion on Men*, National Office of Post-Abortion Reconciliation and Healing.

20. *Description of Aftermath.*
21. *Description of Aftermath.*

Chapter 9. Help and Support

1. Hillary Rodham Clinton, Remarks by Senator Hillary Rodham Clinton to Family Planning Advocates of New York State, January 24, 2005. As included in Melody Rose, *Abortion, A Documentary and Reference Guide* (Westport, Connecticut: Greenwood Press, 2008), p. 244.

2. John C. Willke and Barbara H. Willke, *Why Can't We Love Them Both, Questions and Answers about Abortion* (Cincinnati: Hayes Publishing Company, 1997), p. 270.

3. *Why Can't We Love Them Both*, p. 271.

4. *Why Can't We Love Them Both*, p. 271.

5. www.pregnancycenters.org, Option Line (joint venture between Care Net and Heartbeat International).

6. www.pregnancycenters.org.

7. Heidi Murkoff and Sharon Mazel, *What to Expect When You're Expecting*, 4th Edition (New York: Workman Publishing Company, 2008), p. 59.

8. *What to Expect*, p. 60.

9. *What to Expect*, p. 66.

10. *What to Expect*, p. 66.

11. *What to Expect*, p. 66.

Chapter 10. Choosing Life

1.   Evan Clark, President and Chief Executive Officer of the Department of Commerce Federal Credit Union, April 2008.

2.   South Dakota reference to a fetus as part of its informed consent regulations. "Ruling Gives South Dakota Doctors a Script to Read," *The Washington Post*, July 20, 2008.

3.   Francis J. Beckwith, *Defending Life, A Moral and Legal Case against Abortion Choice* (New York: Cambridge University Press, 2007), p. 164.

4.   www.pregnancycenters.org, Option Line (joint venture between Care Net and Heartbeat International).

Photo Credits and Sources

1. A Sperm Cell Fertilizing an Ovum. Source: Wikipedia (http://en.wikipedia. org/wiki/Spermatazoa).

2. Nuclei of the Sperm and Ovum Dynamically Interact to Form a Zygote. Courtesy of the Carnegie Collection (CC No. 8500.1), National Museum of Health and Medicine, Washington, D.C.

3. The Structure of Part of a DNA Double Helix. Source: Wikipedia (http://en.wikipedia. org/wiki/DNA_double_helix).

4. Eight-Week-Old Embryo. Courtesy of the Carnegie Collection (CC No. 417), National Museum of Health and Medicine, Washington, D.C.

5. 21 Week Male Fetus Grasping Hand of Surgeon. Courtesy of Michael Clancy. See www.michaelclancy.com.

6. Slave Trade Auction Block. Courtesy of Louisiana State Museum, New Orleans, Louisiana.

7. Japanese American WWII Internment Camp. Courtesy of Topaz Museum, Delta, Utah.

8. Ultrasound of 22 Week Fetus. Source: DHD Multimedia Gallery (Anonymous Contributor).

Breinigsville, PA USA
13 March 2011
257505BV00001B/4/P